GOSPEL GOLD
SACRED TREASURES FOR PIANO

GlorySound

A DIVISION OF SHAWNEE PRESS, INC.
EXCLUSIVELY DISTRIBUTED BY HAL LEONARD CORPORATION

Visit Hal Leonard Online at **www.halleonard.com**
and Shawnee Press at **www.shawneepress.com**

Foreword

Embedded deep in the hearts of many singing congregations are the joyful sounds of great gospel music. These classic numbers vibrated to life the spirits of people in good times and in bad. Popularized by music evangelists and gospel quartets, these ageless tunes continue to be the church pianist's most requested numbers because they are reminders of our treasured legacy of praise. These songs can start our toes to tapping and send our hearts soaring. They can bring a tear to the eye or a smile to the face. They are, in fact, golden reminders of the worship of those who came before us and testimonies of joy for those who are just now finding their voice of faith. As you play from this volume, we hope you will enjoy connecting to the cherished music of our gospel traditions and be blessed by the hopeful message that inspired its writing.

Joseph M. Martin
Director of Sacred Publications

Contents

(Alphabetical Order)

Send the Light

Tune: **McCABE**
Music by CHARLES H. GABRIEL
Arranged by
MARY MCDONALD (ASCAP)

SEND THE LIGHT

SEND THE LIGHT

Grace Greater than Our Sin

Tune: **MOODY**
Music by DANIEL TOWNER
Arranged by
PAUL FERRIN (ASCAP)

GRACE GREATER THAN OUR SIN

GRACE GREATER THAN OUR SIN

for Mike and Debbie Christie

When the Roll Is Called Up Yonder

Tune: **ROLL CALL**
Music by JAMES MILTON BLACK
Arranged by
CRAIG CURRY (ASCAP)

Joyful shuffle (rockabilly feel) (♩. = 120-140)

WHEN THE ROLL IS CALLED UP YONDER

WHEN THE ROLL IS CALLED UP YONDER

WHEN THE ROLL IS CALLED UP YONDER

What a Friend

Tune: **CONVERSE**
Music by CHARLES C. CONVERSE
Arranged by JOEL RANEY (ASCAP)

WHAT A FRIEND

WHAT A FRIEND

His Eye Is on the Sparrow

Tune: **SPARROW**
Music by CHARLES H. GABRIEL
Arranged by
MARK HAYES (ASCAP)

Moderately, with expression

HIS EYE IS ON THE SPARROW

HIS EYE IS ON THE SPARROW

HIS EYE IS ON THE SPARROW

HIS EYE IS ON THE SPARROW

HIS EYE IS ON THE SPARROW

to Ruth Sibley

Promised Land

Tune: **PROMISED LAND**
Traditional American melody
Arranged by
JOSEPH M. MARTIN (BMI)

PROMISED LAND

PROMISED LAND

Just a Closer Walk with Thee

Tune: **CLOSER WALK**
Arranged by
PATTI DRENNAN (ASCAP)

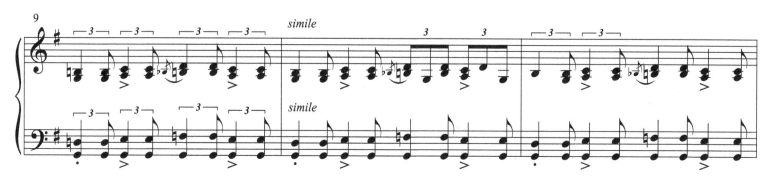

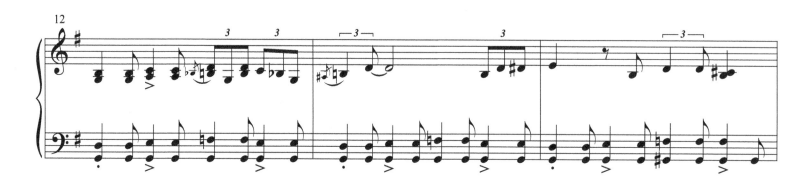

JUST A CLOSER WALK WITH THEE

30

JUST A CLOSER WALK WITH THEE

JUST A CLOSER WALK WITH THEE

'Tis So Sweet to Trust in Jesus

Tune: **TRUST IN JESUS**
Music by WILLIAM J. KIRKPATRICK
Arranged by
HEATHER SORENSON (ASCAP)

'TIS SO SWEET TO TRUST IN JESUS

'TIS SO SWEET TO TRUST IN JESUS

Tho' Your Sins Be As Scarlet

Music by WILLIAM H. DOANE
Arranged by
PAUL FERRIN (ASCAP)

'THO YOUR SINS BE AS SCARLET

Amazing Grace

Tune: **NEW BRITAIN**
Music from Virginia Harmony, 1831
Arranged by
ALEX-ZSOLT (ASCAP)

With feeling (♩ = 72)

AMAZING GRACE

AMAZING GRACE

Like a River Glorious

Tune: **WYE VALLEY**
Music by JAMES MOUNTAIN
Arranged by
LLOYD LARSON (ASCAP)

LIKE A RIVER GLORIOUS

LIKE A RIVER GLORIOUS

LIKE A RIVER GLORIOUS

Stand Up, Stand Up for Jesus

Tune: **WEBB**
Music by GEORGE J. WEBB
Arranged by
CINDY BERRY (ASCAP)

STAND UP, STAND UP FOR JESUS

STAND UP, STAND UP FOR JESUS

Do Lord

Traditional Spiritual
Arranged by
CHUCK MAROHNIC (BMI)

DO LORD

DO LORD

He Keeps Me Singing

Tune: **SWEETEST NAME**
Music by LUTHER BRIDGERS
Arranged by
STAN PETHEL (ASCAP)

HE KEEPS ME SINGING

This Little Light of Mine

African American Spiritual
Arranged by
VICKI TUCKER COURTNEY (ASCAP)

THIS LITTLE LIGHT OF MINE

With abandon

THIS LITTLE LIGHT OF MINE

THIS LITTLE LIGHT OF MINE

Rock of Ages

Tune: **TOPLADY**
Music by THOMAS HASTINGS
Arranged by
ALEX-ZSOLT (ASCAP)

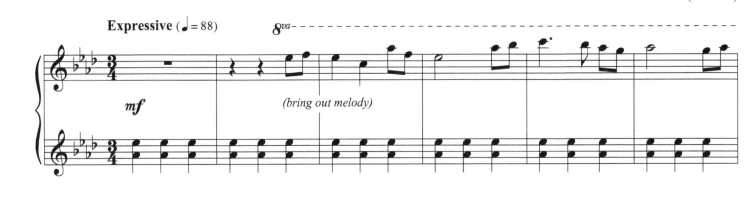

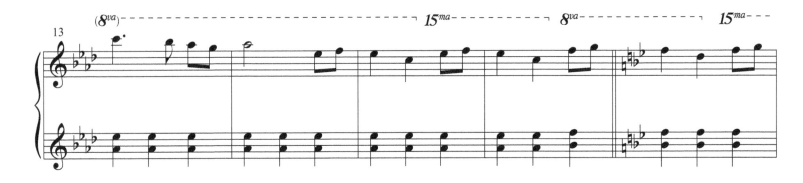

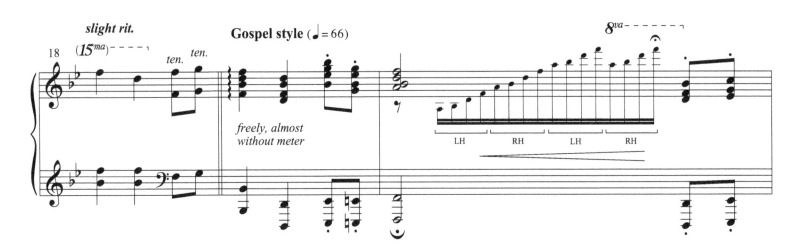

ROCK OF AGES

Going Home

Music by ANTONÍN DVOŘÁK
Arranged by
JOSEPH M. MARTIN (BMI)

Moderately slow and simple

GOING HOME

GOING HOME